THIS BOOK BELONGS TO

....

Edward Lear

EDWARD LEAR

— A —
NEW NONSENSE
ALPHABET

EDITED BY SUSAN HYMAN

BLOOMSBURY

For Elizabeth, Natalya and Rebecca

ACKNOWLEDGEMENTS

For the loan of Leariana and family papers and for their kind
encouragement and advice, the editor would like to thank
James and Rosemary Farquharson. Quotations from Lear's
diary and the preliminary sketches for the Prescott alphabet
are reproduced by permission of the Houghton Library,
Harvard University.

First published in Great Britain 1988

Bloomsbury Publishing Ltd, 2 Soho Square, London W1V 5DE

ISBN 0-7475-0320-6

Designed by Fielding Rowinski
Printed by W. S. Cowell, Ipswich, Suffolk

INTRODUCTION

One of Edward Lear's small admirers recalled in later life the immediate impression created by the 'Laureate of Nonsense': 'I remember perfectly the towering, bearded, spectacled man standing in the drawing-room...and talking in a way which made one feel at once that he was "all right", that is, on the side of the angels—or, as we should probably have expressed it then, the demons—of the nursery and the schoolroom, and in no possible sense a member of the grown-up Opposition. I cannot remember a single word of what he said. There only remains a general, but very strong, pervading sense of well-being and innate rectitude from the standpoint of eight years old. I knew that he was "safe" and that I was safe and that we were all safe together, and that suspicion might at once be put aside.'

Lear's instinctive sympathy for children and their delighted trust in him are widely recorded. Unlike Lewis Carroll, whose interest in his childish intimates diminished with their years, Lear often remained friends with his youthful acquaintances—along with their children, grandchildren, nephews and nieces—for life. Much of his *Nonsense* was composed extempore to divert the children of his hosts, but little is known about the actual circumstances of its creation. The following nonsense alphabet, which has been passed down through generations of the family for whom it was originally drawn, is unusual in being well documented: a draft survives in the Houghton Library at Harvard, and Lear's diaries and letters record both the setting in which it was devised and the affection for a family and its children that inspired it. With slight alterations this alphabet was eventually published in 1871 in *Nonsense Songs, Stories, Botany and Alphabets*.

The genesis of the alphabet can be traced to a meeting on an island in the Ionian Sea. In 1862 Lear was wintering in Corfu, pursuing his combined careers as travel writer and landscape artist. Among his closest friends were Captain Richard Decie, stationed in the British garrison, his wife Bella and their son Frank, also known as 'Merryboy'. Lear was fond of the young couple, frequently dining with them and joining them on expeditions about the island; with an eye trained by early ornithological study, he once observed with mild surprise that 'Mrs Decie hath a Trogon in her hat'. He was sad to see them depart, but the friends were reunited the following June, when Lear too returned to England and visited Bella's parents at Roehampton in Surrey.

There were many subsequent visits to Clarence House—or 'Hospitality Hall', as Lear called it—and the elder couple, William and Arabella Prescott, also became valued friends, patrons of Lear's painting and subscribers to his books. 'I have really never known such people as these,' Lear wrote, 'embodying wealth & simplicity, & immense kindliness.' At their house parties Lear found the sort of cultivated upper-class society in which he thrived, for the Prescotts enjoyed entertaining artists and men of letters; their guests included Tennyson and Thackeray, the Pre-Raphaelites Holman Hunt and Thomas Woolner, the illustrator Dickie Doyle and the excavator of Nineveh, Austen Henry Layard. During the day there were walks through the countryside, croquet and tea in the conservatory, and in the evening, at dinner, good conversation and good wine (Lear wondered if 'Beer, Sherry, Madeira, Hock, Port and Claret, all in one day, are Wrongs').

Lear entertained the children with his nonsense and the adults with his musical settings of Tennyson's poems, and in the privacy of his room he drew, wrote letters and read *The Iliad*. Despite his lack of a formal education, Lear had been brought up on a steady diet of classical myths and had later become proficient in both ancient and modern Greek. He was delighted to find that the rooms at Clarence House were named with the letters of the Greek alphabet. With portentous pseudoscientific nomenclatures and specious suppositions reminiscent of Professor Bosh of 'Flora Nonsensica' repute, he postulates archaeological origins for a wig-stand and a coal-scuttle discovered in Lambda, a cloak-stand described in Theta and a pen-holder in Beta.

On 22 June 1862, Lear noted in his diary: 'Rose at 6:30 & made an alphabet for the Decie baby till 9...lunch at 1:30.—very jovial, hospitable folk!—After this I finished the baby Alphabet till 3:30.' The draft of the alphabet, made during the morning, and the finished alphabet, drawn in deep blue ink on pale blue linen and measuring $12\frac{1}{4}$ by $7\frac{9}{16}$ inches, are reproduced in this book. Many of the creatures in the alphabet derive from Lear's early days as a natural-history illustrator. The innocent and inconsequential verses are nicely devoid of Victorian moral maxims; the 'naughty' rabbit, in particular, is a serenely self-satisfied villain.

Lear made further alphabets that summer for the children of other friends. He wrote to Mrs Prescott, 'Did I tell you that I kept drawing objects for

Alphabets in Yorkshire — & that a domestic nearly fell down with amazement on this order being given him, "Take a cake, an applepie, an eel, a ham and a lobster into Mr. Lear's room, — & afterwards take him to the pump in the courtyard."'

On 9 September 1862 Lear recorded in his diary: 'The Decies have a little girl to whom I wrote.' His letter to Ruth Decie, addressed to 'My dear little tiny child', promises her 'an Alphabet bye & bye', but he warns in a subsequent note to her grandmother, 'Do not let Miss Decie reply to my letter which I sent off today — for too much in writing is not good for her.' Lear's message was a curious, sweet and heartfelt one to send to a new-born baby. The mention of Greek tragedians is not at all gratuitous, for like many comic geniuses, Lear was also a deeply serious man and sadly susceptible to melancholy. In some of the bleaker passages in his diaries he ponders the very question posed by Sophocles: whether 'it is better never to have been born at all, or if born to die as soon as possible'. In his letter he answers the question both for himself and for the infant girl; for this man, who was abandoned by his parents and who never married, took a lover or had children of his own, sustained a belief in the goodness of life and an extraordinary capacity for affection, which endeared him to hundreds of children and adults in his own lifetime and to an infinitude of future devotees of his collected 'vorx of hart'.

The small collection of Leariana that follows celebrates the flourishing of a friendship during a cloudless and apparently ceaselessly comfortable and secure English summer in 1862.

15 Stratford Place. Oxfd St.
9 Sept. 1862

My dear little tiny child,

You will excuse my familiar mode of addressing you, because, you know, – you have as yet got no Christian name –; – & to say – "my dear Miss Decie" would be as much too formal, as "my dear Decie" would be too rude. But as your Grandmama has written to me that you are just born I write to congratulate you, & possibly this is one of the first letters you have as yet received. One of the old Greek Tragedians says—and I am sure you will not think me impertinent in translating what he says—(μὴ φύναι &c) because there has not been time hitherto to buy you a Greek Dictionary, (& I feel sure you cannot read Sophocles without, – besides, the Dictionaries are so fat & heavy I am certain you could not use them comfortably to yourself and your nurse,) – μὴ φύναι &c* – which means "it is better never to have been born at all, or if born, – to die as soon as possible." But this I wholly dissent from : & on the contrary I congratulate you heartily on coming into a world where if you look for it there is far more good & pleasure than we can use up – even in the longest life. And you in particular will find that you have – all quite without any of your own exertions – a mother & a father, – a grandmother & a grandfather, – some uncles, – an extremely merry brother (who propels himself along the floor like a compasses,) a conservatory & a croquet ground, & a respectable old cove who is very fond of small children & will give you an Alphabet bye & bye. – I therefore advise you to live & laugh as long as you can for your own pleasure, & that of all your belongings.

Please tell your Grandmama that I also wished to stop when the carriage passed but couldn't – & say also, that I will write to her again shortly. And now my dear you have read enough for the present. Good night, & believe me,

Your affte old friend

Edward Lear.

Give my love to your Papa and Mama

* *Editor's footnote:* The beginning of a quotation from *Oedipus Coloneus*, 1224–27.

THE
ALPHABET

A

A was some Ants,
Who seldom stood still
And they made a nice house
On the side of a hill.

a.

busy old Ants!

B

B was a Book,
With a binding of blue
And pictures: and stories
For me and for you.

b !

Nice little book !

C

C. was a Cat,
Who ran after a Rat
But his courage did fail,
When she seized on his tail.

C!
Crafty old Cat!

D

D was a Duck,
With spots on his back.
He lived in the water,
And always said Quack!
D,

dear little duck!

E

E. was an Elephant,
Stately and wise,
He wore tusks and a trunk,
And 2 queer little Eyes.

E!
O! what funny small eyes!

F

F was a Fish,
 Who was caught in a net
But he got out again,
 And is quite alive yet.

f!

lively old fish!

G

G was a Goat
Who was spotted with brown.
When he did not lie still,
He walked up and down.

G!
good little goat!

H

H was a Hat
Which was all on one side,
Its crown was too high,
And its brim was too wide.

h!

Handsome old hat!

I

I was some Ice
So white and so nice
But which nobody tasted,
And so it was wasted,
i —
All that good ice!

J

J. was a Jackdaw
Who hopped up and down,
In the principal street
Of a neighbouring town.
J.!
Jacky-jo-jown!

K

K was a kite
Which flew out of sight
Above houses so high
All into the sky.

k!

Fly away kite!

L

L was a Light
Which burned all the night,
And illumined the gloom
Of a very dark room.

l!

Valuable light!

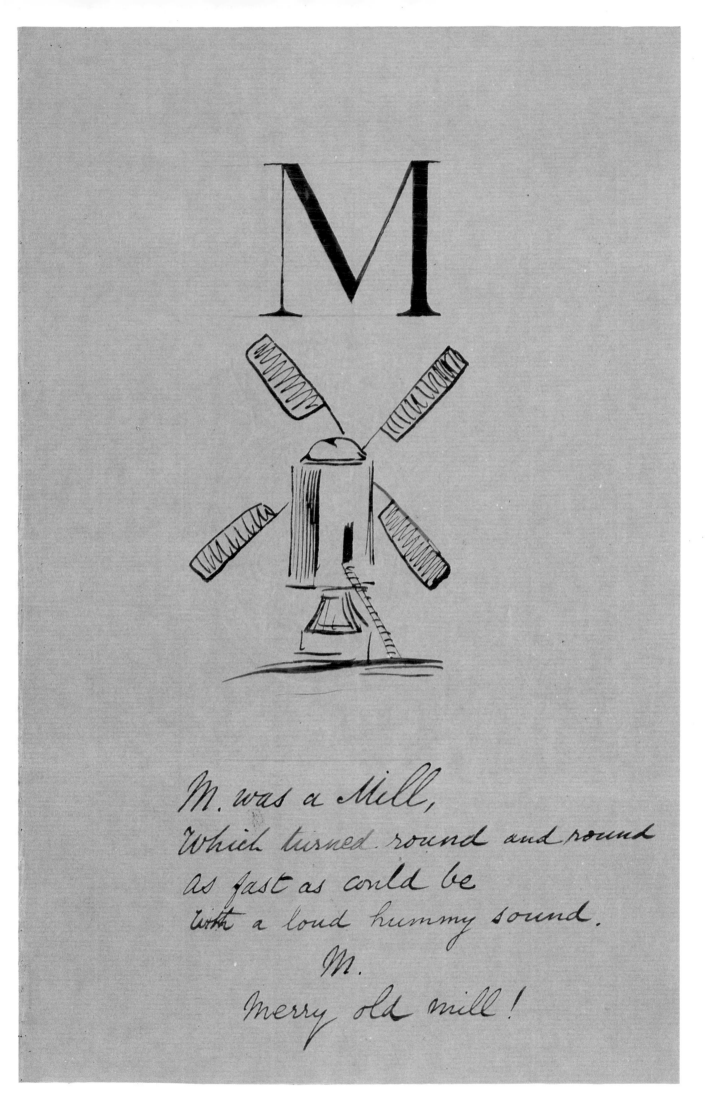

M

M. was a Mill,
Which turned round and round
as fast as could be
with a loud hummy sound.
M.
Merry old mill!

N

N. was a net
Which caught some small fish
And because they were wet
They were put in a dish.

N.

nice little net!

O

O was an Orange
So yellow and round;
When it fell off the tree,
It fell down to the ground.
O!
Down to the ground!

P

P was a Pig
Who was not very big,
But his tail was too curly
And that made him surly.

p!

poor little pig!

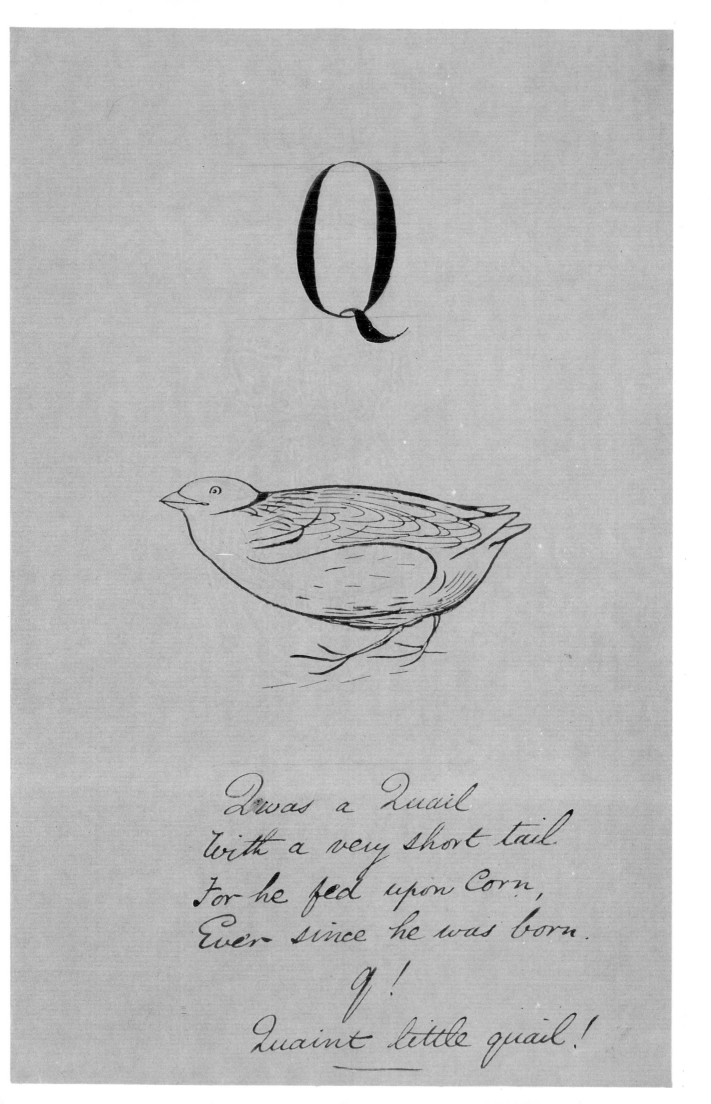

Q

Q'was a Quail
With a very short tail
For he fed upon Corn,
Ever since he was born.

q!

Quaint little quail!

R

R. was a Rabbit
Who had a bad habit
Of eating the flowers,
In gardens and bowers.

r!

naughty fat rabbit!

S

I was a Sugar=tongs,
  Nippity=nee,
To take up the sugar,
  And put in your tea.
          S.
Sugar=go=gee!

T

'Twas a Tortoise,
All yellow and black
But he walked quite away,
And he never came back.

T

torty never came back!

U

U was an Ukase
Kept locked in a Book-case,
And sent by the Czar
To a province afar.

U!

Ugly old Ukase!

V

V. was a villa,
Which stood on a hill,
By the side of a river
And close to a mill.
v.!
Villa and mill.

W

W. was a Whale
With a very long tail
His ways were terrific
Throughout the Pacific!

W.

Remarkable whale!

X. was King Xerxes,
Who more than all Turks is
Renowned for his passion
and furious fashion.
X
Angry old Xerxes!

Y

Y. was a Yew,
Which flourished and grew,
near a quiet abode,
By the side of a road.

y. !

Pretty old Yew !

Z

Z. was some Zinc,
So shining and bright;
Which caused you to wink
In the sun's pretty light.
Z.
Beautiful zinc!
—

THE
SKETCHES

A was some Ants
Who seldom stood still
And they made a nice house
On the side of a hill.   a. Busy old Ants!

B was a Book
With a binding of blue,
And pictures, & stories,
For me & for you.   b. Nice little book!

C was a Cat,
Who ran after a Rat
But his courage did fail
When she seized on his tail.   c. crafty old Cat!

D was a Duck,
With spots on his back.
He lived in the water,
And always said Quack.   d. dear little Duck!

E was an Elephant, stately & wise.
He wore tusks & a trunk, & 2 queer little eyes .   o what funny small eyes.

F was a Fish who was caught in a net
But he got out again, & is quite alive yet ! lively old fish !

G was a Goat, who was spotted with brown
When he did not lie still, he walked up & down.
g . Good little goat —

(house?)

H was a Hat, which was all on one side.
Its crown was too high, & its brim was too wide.
Funny old hat !

I was some Ice
So white & so nice
But which nobody tasted
And so it was wasted . all that good ice !

J was a Jackdaw who hopped up & down
In the principal street of a neighbouring town
J . Jacky go down !

K was a kite
Which flew out of sight
Above houses so high
All into the sky. K ! fly away kite

L was a light, which burned all the night
And illumined the gloom of a very dark room.
l. valuable light!

M was a Mill, which turned round & round,
As fast as could be, with a loud humming sound
Merry old Mill!

N was a Net - which caught some small fish
And because they were wet, they were put in a dish.
n. nice little net.

O was an orange, so yellow & round
When it fell off the tree, it came down to the ground -
o! down to the ground.

P was a Pig, who was not very big
But his tail was too curly, which made him quite surly.
p. poor little pig!

Q was a Quail, with a very short tail
For he fed upon corn, sometimes evening & morn.
q. quaint little quail

R was a Rabbit, who had a bad habit
Of eating the flowers in gardens & bowers, R. naughty fat rabbit!

S. was a sugar tongs, nippetty-nee -
To take up the sugar to put in your tea
Sugar go gee.

T. was a Tortoise, all yellow & black
But he walked quite away,
& he never came back. t. Torty never came back!

U. was an Ukase, kept locked in a Bookcase
And sent by the Czar, to a province afar.
u. ugly old Ukase!

V. was a villa, which stood on a hill.
By the side of a river, & close to a mill -
v. villa & Mill.

W. was a whale, with a very long tail
His _____, were _____, Therefore the
haulfer.
W - remarkable whale!

X. was King Xerxes
Who more than all Turks is
Renowned for his passion
And furious fashion. X
angry old Xerxes.

Y. was a Yew
Which flourished & grew
Near a quiet abode
By the side of a road ... Y Yew!

Z. was some Zinc - so shiny & bright
Wh. caused you to wink, In the sun's
pretty light. z Beautiful Zinc.
Zebra

THE
DISCOVERIES

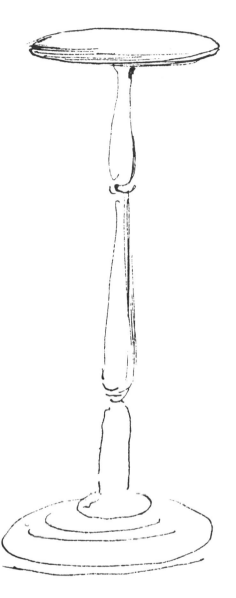

Object, discovered in Lambda.

This remarkable instance of Snumphus, or Peppigrottified Fungus, (growing on a lofty stalk or stem & resembling a Mushroom on Stilts,) has just been discovered in Lambda:– but at the time of our Reporter's departure, nothing was determined as to its previous-present, or past-future condition, nature, or circumstances. Our readers shall however be jooly informed of any further investigations on the topic.

(Eggstract from the Roehampton Chroncile. 16 augt. 1862)

Object: discovered in Lambda, Sept 28. 1862.

We are glad to present our readers with a concise and convalescent illustration of the most remarkable Object discovered in our age – & which is at present causing immense sensation and suffusion in the whole of the civilized world. – This, which is as interesting in its associations as it is singular & beautiful in form, is formed of a jet-like material with devellopments of gold borders all round it & the name "Lambda" in distinct letters on its fulginous face.

The use of the object is at present undetermined; – but it is obvious that it was once, (at an unbeknownly antique period,) the actual property of the illustrious & unfortunate Lambda.

That Lambda is not recorded by any authentic author to have been at Roehampton is advanced by some antiquarians who are desirous of diminishing the value of this priceless object as an objection to this theory: – but it does not follow that Lambda did not send or give the article in question to other persons. – And to all well conditioned individuals the simple fact of Lambda's name being written on the object itself is a full and painful guarantee of its indescribable interest.

Whether the Object in question is Lambda's Snuffbox, or Helmet, or Culinary-pipkin, – or despatch box, time alone, that unveiler of obscure antidotes, – can eventually devellope: – but on those ignorant & disgusting creatures, who have ventured to suggest that this object is a Coalscuttle, no further observation is necessary than that they cannot lay claim to the title of rational human beings, & that they ought to be altogether abolished & prisoned at the earliest aggravating & aggressive opportunity foliowing this notice.

Object discovered in Thêta.
Nov^h. 1. 1862.

It is seldom that we have to call the attention of our readers to so many objects of antiquarian interest, discovered in one spot as the present latest & obviously melancholy article the portrait of which we subjoin, & which has been quite recently discovered in Thêta. Which its origin and use and effect are wholly, (if not almost,) unbeknown to the enlightened & choragic population of the surrounding hemisphere.

On the upper part of the perpendicular & columnar structure of the object is a cross bar – painfully suggestive of the manner in which the amiable Thêta met with her afflicting and philharmonic fate, – (such is the tradition of the country,) – by accidentally mistaking herself for a cloak & hanging herself on the obtrusive Cloak-peg till her futile and invaluable life was extinct. But there are others (it is due to the interests of science to state,) who contend that the singular object in question is the Gigantic & fossil remnant of an extinct brute partaking of the nature of the ostrich & the domestic caterpillar habitually walking on 3 feet, its neck, head and expansive antennae fixed on the summit of its elongated body & its general appearance at once surprising & objectionable.

– Of these conjectures, who shall say which is the true, which is the false, – or which the neither one or t'other?

These doubts cannot be now obspiculated, nor indeed can they entirely be ever expressed. To give our readers an accurate portrait of the Object is our own sole & soporific duty.

Novbr. 1. 1862

Object. Discovered in Beta.
July 11. 1863

We are delighted to acquaint our Readers, (& more especially Harkee! o logical Readers,) that fresh discoveries are on the point of being about to be expected to be supposed to be made at Clarence House, Roehampton, – of which the accompanying drawing represents one of the most interesting hitherto offered to the pusillanimous public. The object in question was found in Beta & is of a indescribable form & indefinable color: and although some idiotic contemporaries have argued that it is intended to hold pens, there cannot be the smallest doubt that it is the stand on which the spears of the remarkable & distinguished Beta were kept when she was not using them. For it is well known that Beta never grew to more that 3 feet 1 inch high, and consequently the penlike but warlike instruments above delineated are quite adapted to her size. Moreover their having been discovered in the apartment which for countless ages has been named after that small but indomitable person, is a parapumphilous proof that requires no other illustration except to the perception of owls, apes, geese, pigs, beetles, or donkies.

Q.E.D.